DEDICATION

I dedicate this book to everyone who was incarcerated.

INTRODUCTION

Life after you are released from prison is not exactly a bed of roses. You are starting over again from scratch, except you have some reserved funds somewhere to draw from. I believe people who are released from prison should get the best possible help and support needed to live peacefully with their families in the society. To do so, reforming your credit and financial standing is mandatory. This book will guide you through the step-by-step process required to get your credit back in the groove.

BELIEVE THAT YOU CAN BOUNCE BACK FINANCIALLY

Every good result is contingent on being positive and believing in its possibility. Your success or failure in reforming your credit begins with your will. You must believe in the possibility that you can be financially stable again despite the odds which seem to be contrary. This will give you strength and focus to climb the ladder towards your financial comeback cum freedom.

BE DETERMINED TO HAVE A CREDIT REFORM AND BE FINANCIALLY STABLE

Determination is a precursor to success. You must tell yourself that no matter what happens, you will persevere on the journey towards your financial restoration. Hear this, result is the by-product of determination

PULL YOUR CREDIT REPORT

Before you can take any step further, it is important that you get your credit report. Only when you have the credit report that you will know how to proceed further. Factors such as your credit check, smart credit and credit karma can be extremely useful for your further steps. So, all you have to do is walk into TransUnion, Equifax or Experian and check your options

LEARN TO READ A CREDIT REPORT

I am not sure reading a credit report would be such an easy task. However, there is nothing to worry about. All you need to do is to learn the basics. Several YouTube videos and resources on the internet can help you learn the basics from the comfort of your home. Learn the fundamentals and take some time to read your credit report.

OPEN A BANK ACCOUNT

You need a bank account to be able to improve your credit scores. Open a savings account in any bank and begin your amazing journey. Remember, staying positive is the most important part of the whole process.

GET YOURSELF AN UNSECURED CREDIT CARD

All you need do is walk into your credit union office and ask for opening an unsecured credit card. The deposit amount varies between $250-3000. Some financial institutions that offer unsecured credit cards are First primer, Capital One, Open Sky, etc.

EXPEDITE YOUR CREDIT SCORES

To establish your credit scores quickly, you need two primary things. Patience and knowing what to do. Find a reliable individual who can provide an authorization for you. Getting the right credit started up is an essential part of the process. After 30-90 days, your credit scores will increase dramatically.

INCREASE YOUR CREDIT

Once you have established a good credit score, you can now go back to the credit union and ask for your credit limit to be increased. Having a great credit score can help you increase your credit limit quickly.

GET A JOB REFERENCE

Try to get a few references from places you have worked in earlier. These references can be an asset to you. However, do not stop if you do not get any references in the initial stages. Hurdles are bound to be there, but with your power and  determination you can get through them quickly.

MAKE A BOLD STEP

Getting a job when you are out from prison is not always an easy task. Begin your life with any job you can get. Do not restrict yourself to any specific type of job. Remember that any job you work hard and earn your living is a great start. Also remember that this is just the beginning. You have a long way to travel.

CREATE ALTERNATIVE INCOME SOURCES

Gone are the days when people are dependent only on one source. On your path to efficient credit reform, you have to create alternative income sources. You can get a sit-at-home jobs as many today survive through freelancing. Learn at least one skill and get things turn to your favor.

ESTABLISH A BUDGET

After getting a job and creating alternative sources of income, it becomes necessary to create a budget to help check for unnecessary expenditure and other excesses such as impulse buying. Stick to your budget even when there is a sudden increase in cashflow coming from external sources, like a tip in your place of work or cash gifts from friends and relatives. Such extra income can be added to your reserve.

KEEP YOUR EXPENDITURE AT MINIMUM

Having gotten a job and established a budget, it becomes imperative to keep expenditures at a minimum. A luxury car or a luxury apartment is good, but timing is everything. Such luxuries are better gotten at the right timing, like when there is a permanent increase in steady income flow such as when there is a change of job to a better job or a job promotion

JOIN A CREDIT UNION

Look for a credit union in your area, if you are not a member of one and make inquiries about joining. You are eligible for a free credit report once a year.

LOOK FOR LOANS

Now that you have a good credit score, all you need to do is look for the right loan. Having good credit scores will provide you the opportunity to utilize personal loans, auto loans, motor loans etc. Find out which loan can help you do better in life.

HAVE A LONG-TERM LOAN REPAYMENT PLAN

The secret to loan repayment in no doubt is having a loan-repayment plan. Formulate a plan and start paying down debt using a budget worksheet

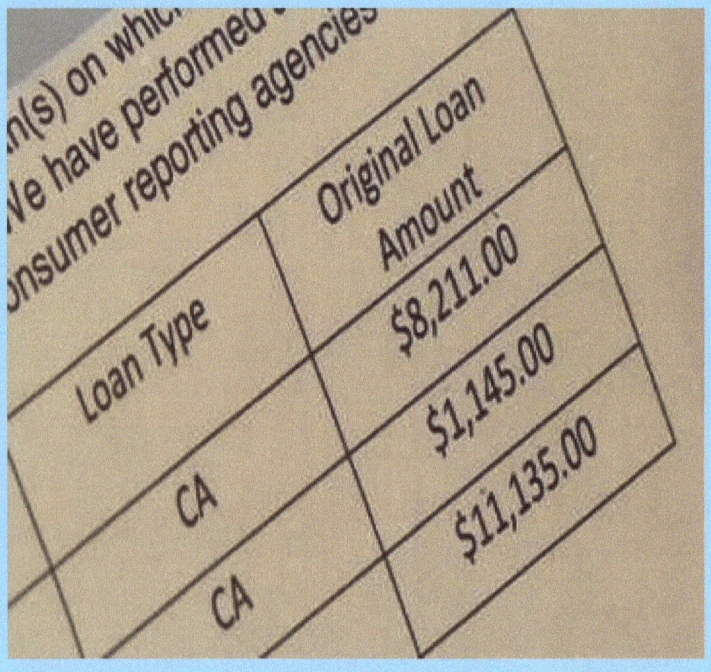

KEEP YOUR DEBT-TO-INCOME RATIO LOW

Should you choose to go for a mortgage plan, endeavor to keep your DTI low. Use a DTI calculation tool to monitor your DTI until it is within a desirable and acceptable range before proceeding for a mortgage.

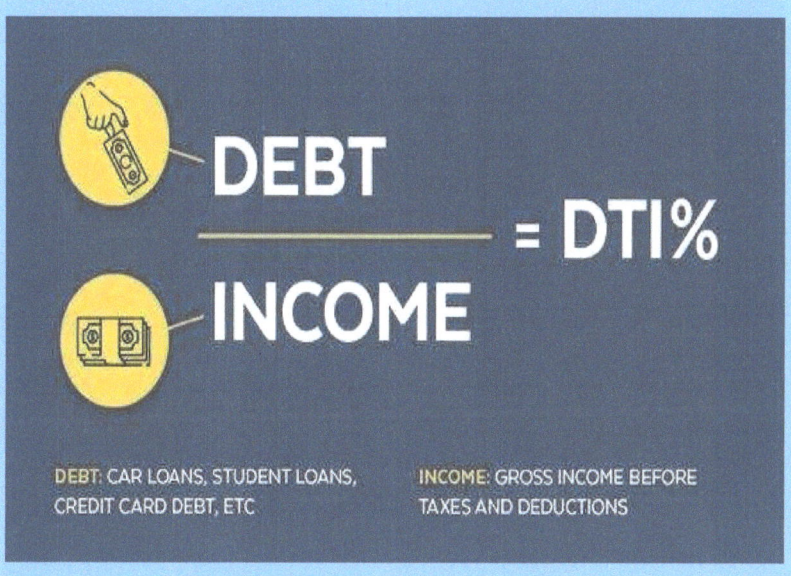

KEEP YOUR RESERVES UP

Put your lender's mind at ease to be sure you can continue to pay your rent in the event of losing your job or experiencing a change in income by keeping your reserves up.

THE SECRET FORMULA

The secret to maintaining a great score is the two-word formula: discipline and leverage. It is always important to build the leverage you built. To do so, all you must do is maintain good discipline by repaying debts on time.

CONGRATS!

Now that you know what to do, I hope you would be a great citizen and be more responsible with your credit scores. Enjoy the life ahead and stay consciously productive. Good luck!

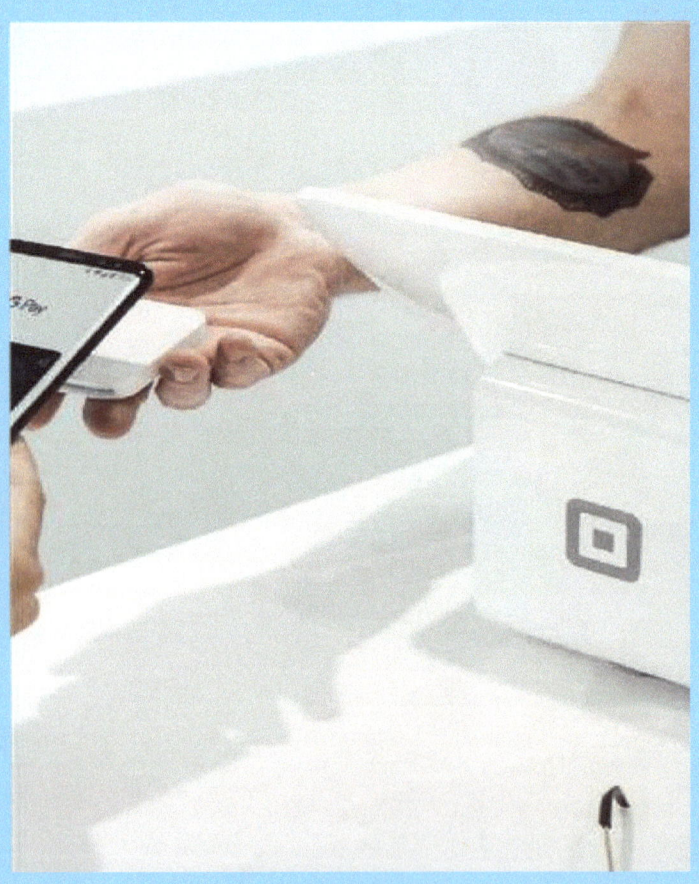

EXPECT MORE

www.ingramcontent.com/pod-product-compliance
Lightning Source LLC
Chambersburg PA
CBHW041945240526
45473CB00033B/613